Breaking Generational CURSES

Robert Strand

E*ergreen
PRESS

Mobile, Alabama

Christmas 2008

ISBN 978-1-58169-286-0
For Worldwide Distribution
Printed in the U.S.A.

Evergreen Press
P.O. Box 191540 • Mobile, AL 36619
800-367-8203

Dedication

To my father,
the Rev. John M. Strand (now deceased)
and my mother, the Rev. Ruth (Strand) Lundeen,
who were excellent mentors and examples
to my two brothers, Gene and Doug,
as well as myself.

Table of Contents

Introduction

IT'S IMPORTANT THAT YOU READ THIS INTRO-DUCTION BEFORE YOU GET INTO THE CONTENT OF THE BOOK ITSELF.

Teaching about family and generational curses is currently quite popular among certain segments of Christianity. But, in this regard, what we believe and how we practice should always be determined by a correct interpretation of the biblical basis of these teachings.

Since I wrote the first book in this series, *The B Word*, I have been invited to return to many places a second or third time to speak on the blessing concepts in more depth. Further study has led me to the subject of this book. It has been a challenging study because of much misunderstanding about the meaning of "gener-ational" or "family curses." I find that much of what has been taught—that a person's guilt is genetically passed down to the third and fourth generation of one's descendants—is actually an incorrect interpreta-tion.

Another error has been that people think they not only inherit the sin nature of an ancestor, but also their accumulated guilt. In other words, they think that God sees them as guilty for their own sins as well as their ancestor's sins. This false teaching even grants Satan the right to hold a claim against any Christian who has not dealt with such generational sins. They reason that, because of this failure, their lifestyle results in all kinds of dire consequences—poverty, shame, impotence, obesity, sickness, grief, poor marriages, fear, lack of success, lack of financial welfare, even early physical death, and on and on.

This thinking leads people to the conclusion that the sacrifice of the blood of Jesus Christ has not been sufficient for them. They think they need to take further action to remove the guilt of an ancestor from an individual in order to live in freedom. This activity can involve all kinds of guilt-removing devices. Some teach a need for a special ceremony in which a person lists the sins of the past four generations and confesses them. Others teach rote prayers or confessions in order to break people free from the past. Some of these teachings go so far as to claim that a Christian has become demon possessed, which is the reason for all their behavioral problems, and so forth.

A careful, honest study of the Bible will show that we are not, I repeat, *not responsible for* the sins of our forefathers and that we are not doomed to see them repeated in our lifestyle! When we look at the point of reference, which Moses used (Exodus 20:5-6; 34:6-7; Numbers 14:18; Deuteronomy 5:9-10; 7:10; 32:41), we need to see the context, especially the statement that the judgment of God falls only on members of the generations "who hate me." It's actually a judgment for people who persist in the rebellious sins against the loving God of their forefathers.

Please understand, first, that the phrase "generational curse" is not to be found anywhere in the biblical accounts. Secondly, the concept of generational curses is foreign when these texts are read in their Near Eastern cultural context. Finally, the so-called "diagnostic" tests or rituals or prayers are simply not found in Scripture. No such steps are prescribed in the Bible, which is the one and only guide for how we are to live and practice our faith.

We must always take in the big picture: In this case, what does the Bible really say about inherited guilt? Just consider one verse which Moses wrote:

The fathers shall not be put to death for the children, neither shall the children be put to death for the fathers: every man shall be put to death for his own sin (Deuteronomy 24:16, KJV).

There are a number of other references in parallel passages, i.e. II Kings 14:6; II Chronicles 25; Ezekiel 18:1-4, 14-20; Jeremiah 31:29-30; Daniel 9:4-5, 7-9; John 8:11, 9:1-3; Romans 14:10-12. These passages, when taken together, reflect a unity of thought that begins with Moses and ends in the teachings of Jesus.

So, why write a book on generational or family curses? One reason is to re-affirm that the sacrifice of Jesus is always sufficient to take care of our past or present. Here's what Paul wrote, without apology:

When you were dead in your transgressions and the uncircumcision of your flesh, He made you alive together with Him, having forgiven us all our transgressions, having canceled out the certificate of debt consisting of decrees against us and which was hostile to us; and He has taken it out of the way, having nailed it to the cross. When He had disarmed the rulers and authorities, He made a public display of them, having triumphed over them through Him (Colossians 2:13-15 NASB).

Another purpose for the book is to demonstrate how to deal with negative "learned" behaviorial patterns from an ancestor and help us to understand that the wrong influence that has been modeled for us can be broken and does not need to be repeated. It is amazing how great the impact—either positive or negative—a man or woman can have on a son or daughter, grandson or granddaughter, or even a great-grandson or daughter.

The ability to transmit ungodly ways to a descendant is limited by the choices of the descendant. We are free to make our own life choices for good or for evil and are responsible for those choices. Further (and this is an encouragement), we are not doomed to repeat the mistakes of our ancestors. Legally or spiritually, we are not responsible for another's sins. We are not genetically bound by any tendencies of those who have gone before us.

There are two types of curses named in the Bible, beginning with Galatians 3:10-13. One is the original curse of sin and the law. This curse Jesus Christ took upon himself at Calvary so that we can go free. The second curse mentioned is the "malediction" (literally, "bad speech"). This is a curse spoken over a person, or an action that is modeled and can be understood as a curse. The sacrifice of Jesus Christ is sufficient to deal with both types. In this book, we'll be dealing with the second type of curse, which can be very real. Please keep the distinction between these two in mind as you read.

This book has a simple message: "If the Son sets you free, you will be free indeed" (John 8:36)! Now let's get on with it!

Never pay back one wrong with another, Or an angry word with another one; Instead, pay back with a blessing. This is what you are called to do, So that you inherit a blessing yourself.

—I Peter 3:9, The Jerusalem Bible

Chapter One

What Is a Generational or Family Curse?

Doris (her name is changed as are all the examples in this book) saw nothing wrong with what was happening to her during her childhood. Ever since she was young, she remembered being touched and fondled by a favorite uncle, her mother's younger brother. This continued into her teen years and then she made a startling discovery—most of her cousins, male and female, had been having the same experience! Tragically nobody in the family ever talked about this abuse! No one was willing to confront it.

As she progressed through her teen years, she

struggled with the possibility of getting some help to stop this behavior. As she gained more understanding, she also grew more determined that something should be done, or at least there should be some kind of intervention. What kept her from going for help? She was afraid of bringing shame on her and her family's reputation, so she kept quiet and bottled all her emotions inside.

However, everything changed when she married and became a mother. Doris decided she could no longer keep this dirty family secret. She broke her silence and went for help in order to protect her child and help her family break out of the bondage.

———◆———

TOO MANY FAMILIES have such secrets, but there is help to become free! Calling such behavior patterns a "curse" may well be the turning point in your own family's well being.

A "curse" has been described as "the damming up of the stream of life." According to Dr./Rev. Sheron Patterson, a generational curse is defined as "a family bondage passed down from one generation to the next." She continues with this clarification, "Many families are unaware that they are caught up in generational curses because it is so normal and natural to them. It's not until they get out into the world and take a good look or get help or counseling that they see their warped, twisted and weird family."

There are any number of negative patterns of behavior which could be considered a curse. These can include physical abuse, emotional abuse, sexual abuse, substance abuse, alcohol abuse, psychological abuse, negative attitudes, sensual life styles, poverty syndromes, and many more. Whatever it happens to be, it can trap a family until futility sets in. Families such as these can become convinced there is no way out!

The rationale might go like this: Great-grandpa was a drunk, grandpa was a drunk, my dad is a drunk, and therefore I have become a drunk. Or, I am a liar because my momma was a real liar, and her mother was a liar, but the worst liar of all was my great-grandma. I'm obese because my parents were obese and their parents were obese and my great-grandparents were obese—so what do you expect? It's in our genes! And on and on it goes.

Such families are bound up in a negative situation that has gone on for so long that it seems as if it is the normal and natural way to live. Divorce can be an action that also fits into this pattern. People with parents who have had multiple divorces not only have multiple divorces themselves, but it seems so do their children. And the beat goes on and on.

———•———

After a meeting where I shared about breaking generational curses, a forlorn looking 19-year-old named Paula approached me with her head down. Softly she whispered, "Can I talk to you?"

"Absolutely."

Head down, with still no eye contact between us, she slowly and quietly began a sad litany. "My mom is a chain-smoker, and now she has lung cancer really bad. I smoke and I want to quit so I don't get sick like her.

"But when I see myself in the mirror, I tell myself the same thing my mother tells me. She says, 'You're just like me—you'll be fat and ugly the rest of your life. You're a loser just like me. You will always be a failure like me. Nobody will ever love you.' She goes on and on, just dumping all her garbage into me."

Paula began to cry softly at first, and then her resolve broke, and she began to sob. "Please help me! I have been cursed by my mother, and now I keep on cursing myself just like she curses me."

"Paula, please look at me," I replied. Slowly, slowly her head came up, and we finally made eye contact.

"Thank you, now listen carefully. There is help for you! Can you believe it is possible for you to change?"

There was a slight nod of her head and a quiet, hesitant whispered, "Yes."

"You're not alone . . . there is help," I affirmed to her.

"Yes," another pause, and she couldn't help but add, "I'm a real mess."

Here was a daughter of Christ who was devastated by her own mother. My heart ached for her. "Let's begin with a promise from God's Word," I began. "The Bible says, 'Christ redeemed Paula (us) from the curse of the law by becoming a curse for Paula (us) . . . He redeemed Paula (us) in order that the blessing given to Abraham might come to Paula (the Gentiles) through Christ Jesus, so that by faith Paula (we) might receive the promise . . .' Here's the beginning. Christ became a curse in our place—in your place—Paula!" I concluded.

A tiny smile began to form. Almost afraid to believe such great news, she asked, "Does it *really* say that?"

"Yes . . . well, not exactly. I mean your name isn't really written in the Bible," I admitted. "But the truth is that Christ Jesus became a curse and your name is implied as well as mine, and the names of all people for all time. He takes your curse away because of His sacrifice on the cross. Do you believe it?"

Hope and fear flashed alternately across her face. "Yes . . . but . . ."

"But what?" She was so close to a new life. I prayed she would hear the good news that would free her from the garbage in which she lived.

"Is this for real? Where is it in the Bible?" she asked, trying not to appear too eager.

"Here, look with me at Galatians 3:13-14. It was written as truth for you for your situation:

> *Christ redeemed us from the curse of the law by becoming a curse for us, for it is written: 'Cursed is everyone who is hung on a tree.' He redeemed us in order that the blessing given to Abraham might come to the Gentiles through Christ Jesus, so that by faith we might receive the promise of the Spirit.*

"This promise is for you, Paula, and you can apply it with a simple act of faith—just simply believe it. With this truth you can begin a life that is new and special."

She looked at me, a tiny tear slipping from her eye and a smile of acknowledgment beginning to form. "It's really that simple?"

"Yes. Now, what will you do with this from today on?" I challenged her.

"Well, for starters, when I look into the mirror I will not curse myself. I can't stop my mom from cursing me, but I will not curse myself anymore."

"Way to go Paula ... there's a whole lot more, but it begins with this positive promise. No more cursing yourself is the first step!"

Paula walked away with her head high and a bit of bounce in her step, probably for the first time in her life.

HOW DOES THE BIBLE EXPLAIN or define a "curse"? The study of "a" curse or "the" curse can be quite extensive because the word appears more than two hundred times in the Bible. There are several Hebrew (Old Testament) and Greek (New Testament) words that are simply translated as "curse." They all basically imply the same thing, with various shades of meaning.

For example, such Hebrew words in the Old Testament as: *naqab, qabab, qalal, taalah* and *arar* are all translated as forms of the word curse—curses or cursed or cursing. The basic root meaning is almost identical. They are written to describe the word "curse," as "to make something accursed; to adjure in a bad sense; to puncture or perforate with the violence of words; to malign; to execute; to stab with words; to bring someone into contempt; to despise; to vilify; an imprecation; to execrate another or to bitterly curse." It's interesting in that it takes more than a single word or phrase to describe the biblical meaning of the English word "curse."

In the New Testament, it's much the same. A number of words are all translated as "curse," which include: *kataron, keramikos,* and *anathematizo.*

7

Collectively their meanings are "an imprecation, to doom, to revile, to speak evil of, to declare or vow an execration, to bind another under a curse, to bind with an oath, and to speak evil of."[2] It's not a pretty picture.

There are a number of recorded instances of cursing in the Scriptures. God cursed the serpent, who had seduced Eve to eat of the special tree in the Garden of Eden (Gen. 3:14). He also cursed Cain who murdered his brother Abel (Gen. 4:11). God cursed the ground so it would produce weeds and to make it hard work to till the ground until it produced a crop (Gen. 3:17-19). God also promised to curse anyone who cursed Abraham (Gen. 12:1-3). These divine pronouncements, future prophecies, or maledictions were more than mere words. These divine words carried effects that were long term.

We can also find a listing of twelve curses that can be self-inflicted because of faulty behaviors or actions (Deut. 27:15). There is a curse down to the third or fourth generations of those who hate God (Ex. 20:5-6). Then, too, curses were delivered by holy men (Gen. 9:25; 49:7; Deut. 27:15; Josh. 6:26) and were more than expressions of revenge. These were predictions or future prophecies.

The Bible forbade the cursing of one's mother or father (Exod. 21:17) on the pain of death. They were also not to curse a leader or prince (Exod. 22:28) or even a person who is deaf (Lev. 19:14). Cursing God was a capital crime (Lev. 24:10). Pretty heavy stuff.

In more modern vernacular, a curse can best be described as a "whammy, damnation, execration, denunciation, imprecation, blasphemy, swearing, burden, tribulation, torment, plague, scourge, a cross to bear, cuss, blast, condemnation, and vexation."[3]

But when God comes on the scene, He can and will turn the curse into a blessing! A blessing is the opposite of a curse. When you are blessed you are "made holy, anointed, ordained, filled with grace, filled with joy, experiencing God's favor, protected, endowed, supported, watched over, blissful, wonderful, fortunate, favored and graced!"[4] In contrast to the word "curse" in all its forms, which appears some two hundred times in the Bible, the word "bless" in all derivations appears more than five hundred times!

Twice as much content is spent on the blessing in contrast to the opposite. There's an important principle here for all of us!

---

[1] *The Exhaustive Concordance of the Bible*, James Strong, S.T.D., L.L.D., Abingdon Press, Nashville.

[2] Ibid.

[3] *Unger's Bible Dictionary*, Merill F. Unger, Moody Press, Chicago.

[4] Ibid.

Study Guide

Chapter 1: Ask yourself, "What do I need to do first?"

1. In the story of Doris, what is the turning point?

_____

_____

_____

2. Is there a key for changing my behavior?

_____

_____

_____

3. How do I define a family or generational curse?

_____

_____

_____

4. What are the family curses I am dealing with right now?

_____

_____

_____

5. What do I see as hope for my current situation?

_____

_____

_____

6. The first step I will take is:

_____

_____

_____

In my living, I can make any life choices I want and desire.

But what I cannot do is choose my consequences!

—Randy Nelson,
Pastor of Patchwork Church,
Belton, MO

Chapter Two

How Is a Generational
Curse Passed On?

How does it happen? Simple . . . people imitate what they see modeled for them. It's called "learned behavior."

One generation can fall into a bad habit or negative situation and never are able to break it or get out of it. They wind up internalizing it in the family system. It happens. Then the generations coming after them follow the same behaviorial patterns.

The following is an example of how learned behavior can be passed on. A young man married into a family that had an interesting way of preparing a roast or ham for the Sunday dinner. After the honeymoon, and the first big meal in their humble apartment was being prepared, the new groom noticed this peculiarity. His bride cut off both ends of the roast before putting it the roasting pan. He thought it was strange and wasteful of good meat, so he asked, "Honey, why did you cut off the ends of the roast?"

She looked at him and replied, "I don't know, but my mother always prepares a roast like this."

The next time they visited at the home of his in-laws, he observed his mother-in-law preparing a roast for dinner, and she too cut off the ends of the roast. He asked, "Mom, why did you just cut off both ends of the roast?"

She gave him a puzzled look and replied, "I'm not sure, but my mother always fixed her roasts just like this."

Finally, they made a visit to grandmother's house. And sure enough as she was fixing the roast for dinner, she cut off both ends of the roast. The new grand-son-in-law in the family asked, "Grandma, why did you just cut off both ends of the roast? You are wasting all that good meat."

She looked at him and said, "Oh, my roasting pan is smaller than the roasts."

This is also the way in which positive behavior patterns are passed down from one generation to the next.

Dr. Charles W. Johnson, clinical psychologist, says that a generational curse is a cycle that reflects a pattern of "disconnection, disaffection, and dysfunction." He also adds, "It's a trans-generational perpetuation of a pattern of behavior that has an oppressive grip on a too sizable proportion of our communities."

Both negative and positive patterns are caught as they are modeled and taught.

Both negative and positive patterns are caught as they are modeled and taught. Certain behaviors are learned just by watching others, especially important others such as parents, family and relatives.

Childhood is the most crucial, critical period in the shaping of a child for life. Every child needs at least one positive adult parent who is modeling the best behaviors on which to base a positive lifestyle! Two positive parents are better. Two positive parents plus a positive, supportive extended family are the best. Their impact can also be strengthened by attendance at a supportive, positive, uplifting, loving church. It's even better when the school also is an excellent support system. And the very best is when the community and nation model this better behavior. You see, it's more caught by the young than it is taught to them!

Positive, loving Christian persons will reflect to their children that they are worthwhile and lovable and will become responsible citizens in their world. On the other hand, too many children have parents and family members who are operating from a distorted, cracked and fragmented lifestyle so they can't reflect to the child a positive view of life.

I have been told that psychologists, in studying "learned behaviors," have used an experiment with a rat and a maze. Let's take time to observe it.

⸺•⸺

The starting point of the maze is wired so that it delivers a shock to the rat, who then is highly motivated to enter the maze, frantically looking for a way out.

The rat is poised on the starting point and suddenly a mild electric shock is administered. Out jumps the rat, which immediately searches for an escape. Finally he stumbles on an open door, and entering it, finds a reward—a bit of cheese. He nibbles the cheese and is lifted back to the starting point. The shock again is administered, but this time the rat more quickly finds the open door and the reward. The next time he's really quick. The fourth time he's even quicker, and by the fifth time the shock is given to the rat, it's as though he were on a racetrack with a reward waiting for him.

Then the door leading to the cheese was shut. The rat is shocked into his run to the door, but it's closed. The rat smashes into the closed door and wanders in confusion. He's returned to the starting point, but this time is much slower on his trip to the open door and the anticipated reward. Again he is confused at the closed door. He's brought back to the starting point, shocked again, and makes his way extremely slowly to the closed door, only to be disappointed once more. Finally, the rat is on the starting point and shocked, and shocked, and shocked. The rat refuses to even try. The poor rat can be shocked to death but refuses to budge. This rat has learned failure. He's learned defeat. He's learned that it would be no more use for him to even try. He's learned helplessness!

GOD IS THE DOOR OPENER! He's our way out from doors that have been slammed in our faces! It might be a tragedy, but too many people have learned helplessness and become victims of the system of behavior in which they find themselves trapped. You may be one of those people who are looking for a way out but have given up because any hope of change is gone.

I'll say it again: God is the door opener! He's the way out of our maze of learned helpless behavior! Generational and family curses can be broken. Habits can be stopped, and with God's help we can stop the cycle! Yes, we can do it!

God is very interested in what happens from one generation to the next generation in a family. Carefully read the following verses with me,

> *For I, the LORD your God, am a jealous God, punishing the children for the sin of the fathers to the third and fourth generation of those who hate me, but showing love to a thousand generations of those who love me and keep my commandments* (Exodus 20:5-6).

Note that the punishment is for generations of those who hate God, those who reject God, those who refuse to keep His commandments. But God shows love to a thousand generations of those who love the Lord and keep His commandments. Please keep this distinction in mind. It's quite simple. You can ask yourself: Am I a part of a generation that loves or hates the Lord? This can be a moment in your life to turn from hate to love because of the benefits to the generations following you.

———•———

Walt was a good man, a generous man, except for one thing—he had an absolutely uncontrollable temper. He was a dairy farmer, and even his cows lived in fear of him. More than once I observed when a cow didn't do what she was supposed to do, he'd grab anything handy—a 2 x 4 board, a milking stool, or a pitchfork—and beat the cow until she'd quiver with fear.

His wife and two sons lived in a constant state of never knowing when or what would set him off. He'd beat his boys at the slightest excuse. He never physically hit his wife, but he abused her vocally. He was known in that part of the county as a man you should not cross. In a fit of rage one day, he killed a wonderful cattle dog with his shotgun.

One time, because his new Studebaker Commander refused to start, in anger he grabbed a nearby five-pound maul and beat in the driver's side door, smashing in the windshield before he stopped. He was a man who was completely out of control.

Sadder still was that one of his two sons was also out of control. His excuse—"I'm just like my dad." In high school he became a brawler. He was thrown off the basketball team because of his temper. He also had a hair-trigger reaction. The other son took after his mother with a much more even personality.

Then one day a real tragedy occurred. The older son became irritated with a rival over a girl. In a fit of anger he grabbed the shotgun from the gun rack in his pick-up and shot this rival who was a long time friend because he had attempted to court the same girl. Fortunately, he didn't kill his friend, who managed to survive after a prolonged hospital stay.

In the courtroom, he pleaded guilty to charges of assault with a deadly weapon. Before the sentence was passed, the judge asked, "Do you have anything to say?"

There was silence. Then his dad, Walt, stood and pleaded with the judge for lenience because this son was not at fault. Walt said, "It's because of the way I have lived before my son that he too learned how to erupt in a fit of rage whenever he was crossed. I taught him how to settle any problems—just get mad and let it out. I should be the one sentenced."

By the time he was finished, Walt was in tears and sat down with his face in his hands and sobbed like a baby.

———•———

THAT'S A SAD STORY WITH A SAD ENDING. However, you still have time to change the ending of your story or your family. This is about making new and better choices. How we live and what we model is important to those who come after us. Words and actions have meaning and consequences. There is help, and there is hope! After you work through the study guide on the next page, let's read on in the next chapter as to some specific positive steps you can take, beginning now.

STUDY GUIDE

Understanding how a curse is passed to the next generation.

1. What is "learned" behavior?

_____

_____

_____

2. Why do you think it is so easy for "modeled" life actions to be duplicated?

_____

_____

_____

3. Why do you think we are so easily influenced by people we live with?

_____

_____

_____

4. Who in your family has modeled a damaging life style?

_____

_____

_____

5. What behavior patterns in your life should be changed or modified?

_____

_____

_____

Sing, O Daughter of Zion; shout aloud, O Israel!

Be glad and rejoice with all your heart, O Daughter of Jerusalem!

The Lord has taken away your punishment, he has turned back your enemy.

The Lord, the King of Israel, is with you; never again will you fear any harm.

The Lord your God is with you, he is mighty to save.

He will take great delight in you,

He will quiet you with his love,

He will rejoice over you with singing.

—Zephaniah 3:14-15,17

Chapter Three

Practical Steps To Take

Mike told me, "I still hear my dad telling me, 'YOU are a dummy! YOU are a loser! YOU will never amount to anything!' And there was much, much more he said to me. Here I am, fifty-five years old, and I still hear his voice as fresh in my mind and soul as when he said it. It's like a tape or CD constantly going on inside my head.

"The worst part is especially when I want to do something new with my life. It's a constant battle. Now he's dead and gone, and I can't talk to him or hear him tell me something better.

"But today, for the first time I have hope that this

can be turned around. I'm going to do what you just told me. I believe there is a way out of my trap. With God's help and the help of my wife, I'm going to start something new. With this new understanding, I can break free of my past. I know it!"

———•———

YES, THERE'S HOPE for Mike and all of us who feel trapped by our past histories. Together we can take positive action to move toward the blessing. The following are some practical, simple steps we can use as tools to help us break free from the bondage of the past.

1. Before it can be fixed, face it.

Here's the starting point. Perhaps you have never taken a long hard look at your situation or the situation in your family. Be honest. Listen to those quiet warning signals inside that are telling you something is very wrong. God has placed a conscience in each of us. So if you quiet yourself, you may discover God is still at work and has some wisdom to give you. There is that something in all of us, if we have not completely squashed it, that tells us right from wrong.

> **It's never too late to take charge.**

Don't go creating a problem if there isn't one. But if there is, and you have become aware of it, it's never too late to take charge. When you make the decision to deal with the problem, no matter how difficult and no matter how long it has gone on, you will have taken a significant step. In fact, this may the biggest battle in dealing with these issues that you will face. The problem cannot be dealt with, nor can you experience freedom in your situation, unless you recognize it for what it is. It's a problem or situation that needs to be fixed.

2. Tell someone about it—honestly talk it out.

Who is someone you can really trust? Do you have an understanding friend? Do you have a family member who would give you a listening ear? Perhaps you have a counselor, pastor, or mentor who is this kind of person.

Women seem to be much better equipped to more easily take this step. Men may have a bit more difficulty in opening up to someone else. But it's important. Two are better than one when facing serious situations. There's help in numbers, but you don't have to tell the world. You just need one or two people who will be helpful and supportive in your battle for freedom and release from bondage. The best would be someone who understands and will be there in prayer support. It should be someone you can lean on and in whom you can confide.

3. Act quickly.

Do it the sooner the better because immediate intervention is the key, before anger, cynicism, helplessness, and bitterness stop your momentum. You need to stop the cycle before your heart again grows hard and your defenses are erected.

Now that you've taken the first two steps, it's too soon to give up, even though you might be tempted to throw in the towel at this stage. It's here that many get cold feet. Maybe we think too much. We wonder, *What will people say? I really don't want to hurt so and so. Will I still be able to hold my head up in good company?* The questioning and second-guessing may throw up barriers to your freedom. Do it now!

4. You need to take control of your situation.

You do not have to keep on being the victim. At first, you may be blindsided and caught off guard. The next time, do all in your power to prevent it from happening again. You may have to stay away from certain situations. You may have to resist habitual thoughts. It may involve taking a whole new course of action, but only you can take the necessary action.

You make the decision, and God will give you the grace and power to pull it off. But until the decision is made and converted into action, nothing changes. You may have attempted to resist before, but failed because you felt totally helpless and intimidated. Today is a new day with a new opportunity. Don't give up at this stage in your journey to be free!

5. Call a wrong a wrong and a sin a sin.

Difficult? Yes, this takes a lot of guts. But again, I remind you that, with God's help, all things become possible. Just know that the first time you do this may be the hardest. But the Bible tells us that if we cover our sins we will not prosper. The cover-up simply allows the situation to continue and maybe even to escalate to another level. Yes, this may have gone on way too long and nobody has ever intervened, but the time has come to do something about it.

You may be thinking, *This is too hard. I am afraid it may trigger angry responses from the perpetrator.* Did anybody say this would be easy? Not me, and if you are honest, not you, either. Perhaps intense fear will try and smother you. Again I remind you, love is the antidote to fear. Who is the real source of love? The Bible tells us that God is love! You need Him to walk with you through this trial. Be assured that when you call on Him, He will answer!

6. Turn away from the person or situation.

Maybe this is the critical time in your life to find new friends or, at the least, not hang around with those who have been abusing you. Tough to do? Yes.

But remember, you have the help you need for the asking.

You may need to go outside of your present circle to create a new support system of friends or relatives. You may not be happy about this, but this action may be the key to your future. Drastic situations demand drastic actions. You may even need to go so far as to think about relocation.

7. Stop keeping family secrets.

The big deal is that families do keep secrets. Maybe it's time to talk this situation out with one or both of your parents (if they are available, sympathetic, and not involved) with the hope that they may be able to share with you what and why this has become a pattern. Silence only keeps an evil cycle going in the household. It's time for you to put your "tough love" into action!

There you have it: a simple step-by-step plan to break the pattern! It's nothing more profound than using and acting on common sense. The truth is that no one can do this for you. If you determine that your actions have brought a curse upon you, then determine that your actions can go a long way toward breaking and stopping the problem!

There is a story told in Israel about a novice rabbi who was a bit frustrated because he wasn't given the respect in the village where he lived. He believed himself to be wise and worthy of their respect, but the villagers didn't give it to him. So he became bitter.

He wanted to exact a bit of revenge on them when an old, wise, and highly respected rabbi visited the village. He conceived a plan. He would catch a small bird and hold it in his hand and ask the rabbi if the bird were alive or dead. If the rabbi said "alive," he would squeeze the bird to death and hold it out for all to see. If the rabbi answered "dead," he would open his hand and let the bird fly. Showing the rabbi up, he reasoned, would give him the respect he should be accorded.

The next day as the older rabbi was teaching among the villagers, the brash young man challenged him. "Rabbi, we know you are wise, but can you tell me? Is the bird in my hand alive or dead?"

The older rabbi was silent for a few moments. A hush fell over the crowd as the villagers leaned forward to hear his answer. He looked at the young rabbi, and with love and gentleness, he replied, "The answer is up to you."

THE SAME THING HOLDS TRUE TODAY for you and me. What will you do with the choices that face you at this moment? Will you make a choice to bring blessing into your life, or will you continue in a situation that curses you? We can curse the past and continue to be a victim, or make a choice to bring blessing into our living! It's your choice . . . It's my choice . . . It's our choices.

In the next chapter we'll bring the power of the blessing of God into this mix. Here's where breaking the curse really gets exciting!

Study Guide

1. What steps should be taken as I move towards freedom?

_____

_____

_____

2. Which of the above steps might seem to be the hardest to take?

_____

_____

_____

3. Why?

_____

_____

_____

4. Can you think of something more to be added to these seven steps?

_____

_____

_____

5. What will you do if you are rejected when you attempt these actions?

_____

_____

_____

6. How will you implement any or all of these steps?

_____

_____

_____

7. When do you plan to begin?

_____

_____

The neatness of a theory may be no match for the messiness of reality!

—*Donna M. Strand, counselor*

Chapter Four

The Blessing That Breaks the Curse

Let's begin with one of the most powerful biblical passages on dealing with curses that may have been placed on your life by others. Historically, the children of Israel, under the fabulous leadership of Moses, had come out of hundreds of years of slavery. They crossed the Red Sea and lived for forty years in one of the world's most desolate and inhospitable deserts on this earth.

Life wasn't easy. They were dealing with their painful past and some present problems. For one thing, nobody came to help them while they were in their desert wanderings. None of the inhabitants offered assistance, not even food or water. In fact, two groups of people even hired a sorcerer to place a curse on them.

These people groups, the Ammonites and Moabites, hired Balaam to pronounce a curse on the Israelites. But read how God responded to the attempted curse:

> *However, the Lord your God would not listen to Balaam but turned the curse into a blessing for you, because the LORD your God loves you* (Deuteronomy 23:5).

The Lord...turned the curse into a blessing because the Lord your God loves you.

God's love for His people reversed the curse! It no longer was a curse—it became a blessing! What a wonderful thought: because the Lord your God loves you! Do you think God loved the Israelites any more than He loves you today?

This is absolutely awesome! Here's the promise to depend upon, pray with, and declare your freedom on. You can build your future on this foundational promise. If God did it in the past, He can do it in the present. It's the principle of the blessing at work in your life. I say, "DO IT AGAIN, LORD!"

The blessing can be a mystery, but this one thing we do know from reading God's Word—it works! It's like being kissed with the favor of God! The blessing brings you release from the past so you can experience a new start. This blessing of God enables you to do what you could not do before it was released by faith into your situation.

The blessing is your permission to rise to a new level of living! Jesus blessed His followers by declaring that they were "...the salt of the earth ...the light of the world ...a city on a hill," so that all could see. At the time of these declarations, their lives represented none of these things, but they rose to the level of the blessing and became the people that blessed the world.

In Deuteronomy 28, you can see that there's a night and day difference between living with the blessing or living under a curse. This passage lists twenty-eight specific blessings that are yours when you live in obedience to God's plan. The curses for disobedience are also outlined. It's this matter of "choice" once again. Live in obedience and...

All these blessings will come upon you and accompany you if you obey the Lord your God (Deuteronomy 28:2).

You may not even be aware of these blessings; they will just accompany you on your life's journey. On the other hand, disobedience triggers the opposite effect...

*However, if you do not obey the Lord your God
...all these curses will come upon you and
overtake you* (Deuteronomy 28:15).

You cannot run fast enough to avoid the consequences, either positive or negative. The choice is
yours.

The following twenty-eight blessings, are written in
a condensed easy-to-remember form.

The Blessings of God

1. Promotion...

2. The favor of God, the favor of others...

3. Be blessed in the city...

4. Be blessed in the country...

5. Offspring of children...

6. Good crops...

7. Strong cattle...

8. Fertile cattle...

9. Fertile flocks...

10. Quality fruit to harvest...

11. Prosperous homecomings...

12. Prosperous travels...

13. Victory in life's battles ...

14. Deliverance from danger...

15. Overflowing storehouses...

16. Prosperous business...

17. Prosperous family ventures...

18. Fertile land...

19. Sanctification...

20. A calling by God's name...

21. Security...

22. Riches...

23. Timely rain...

24. Meaningful work...

25. You will facilitate lending...

26. Eliminate borrowing...

27. Experience leadership...and

28. Life success!

That just pretty well covers all of our life's needs. What possibilities! What a God! What blessings!

There's much more that you need to understand about the power of the blessing to change your life for the better. The New Testament gives us the most powerful concepts regarding the blessing. Let's look at how it works in reality.

By Faith

Let me first ask you a question or two. What action did you take to become a Christian? How do any of us receive a healing from the Lord? How is it possible to daily live the Christian lifestyle?

"By faith" should be your answer to these three questions. Let's investigate how faith works when it comes to the blessing of God in your life.

*Consider Abraham: "He believed God and it was credited to him as righteousness." Understand, then, that **those who believe are children of Abraham*** (Galatians 3:6-7 emphasis added).

Here's the significance—those who believe are! Present tense! In the now! Believers are!

Now we move on to the next affirmation,

Clearly no one is justified before God by the law, because "The righteous will live by faith" (v. 11).

There can be no question that faith is absolutely

necessary to live the Christian life. Faith is not some kind of hocus-pocus. It's a deliberate action. It's something simple and straightforward.

What are the exact elements of faith that are necessary to believe? The Bible, being the best commentary on itself, shares the answer with us in the "faith" chapter, Hebrews 11:6,

> And without faith it is impossible to please God, because anyone who comes to him must believe that he exists and that he rewards those who earnestly seek him.

So what is faith and how much of it do you need to become part of the family of God or to receive help from God? It's easy. Do you believe God exists? Excellent! Secondly, do you believe He rewards those people who earnestly petition Him? Right on! There are no mysteries in faith. It's so simple that even a child can understand it. There are two elements: Believe God is—that He exists—and that He rewards all who earnestly seek Him! It's simple; don't make it too difficult. I have digressed, let's get back on track and move on in regard to the blessing.

The next step is important for you to really understand. Galatians 3:13 means exactly what it says,

> Christ redeemed us from the curse [including all family or generational curses] by becoming a curse for us.

43

What is "the" curse? It's sin in any shape or form. Believe it, my friend, Jesus Christ once and for all time has redeemed us from the curse, including any past, present, or future family or generational curses. This includes any all time, all-inclusive curse of any kind! The sacrifice of Jesus Christ is sufficient. There is nothing more that needs to be added to set you free from the past! I don't need to understand how it was that He became a curse for each of us, I just take it on faith. It happened! It's finished! You have been set free; now all you do is accept this ultimate sacrifice by faith.

But there's more. He redeemed us to set us free from the curse, and He also redeemed us for another purpose:

He redeemed us in order that the blessing given to Abraham might come to the Gentiles [that's us] *through Christ Jesus, so that by faith we might receive the promise of the Spirit* (Galatians 3:14).

What is "the blessing" given to Abraham by God? It seems unbelievable, but this same blessing is available to all of us. Here it is from the Old Testament:

God said, "I will make you into a great nation (family) and I will bless you; I will make your name great, and you will be a blessing. I will bless those who bless you, and whoever curses you I will curse; and all peoples on earth will be blessed through you" (Genesis 12:2-3).

Awesome! The blessings and benefits of God in the life of Abraham were absolutely enormous. The blessing enabled him to do and become something he could not have done or been before the blessing of God in his life. And, my friend, this blessing is promised to you with all its ramifications and possibilities! (I'll deal in more depth with the implications of the blessing in another chapter.)

The key to living with and in the blessing is that it is triggered by your faith. Now in case you and I haven't understood how this is to happen, the Bible clarifies it with the following explanation. The Apostle Paul wrote this to the Galatian church:

The Scripture declares that the whole world is a prisoner of sin, so that what was promised being given through faith in Jesus Christ, might [will] be given to those who believe *(Galatians 3:22).*

There's the theme re-stated so that none of us can misunderstand the simplicity of the blessing. The writer returns in a final paragraph to tell us:

You are all sons [and daughters] of God through faith in Jesus Christ . . . and have clothed yourselves with Christ. There is neither Jew nor Greek, slave nor free, male nor female, for you are all one in Christ Jesus. If you belong to Christ, then you are Abraham's seed, and heirs according to the promise (Galatians 3:26-29).

If you are a person who thinks the blessings of God are for a privileged few, Paul has removed all distinctions of race, color, status, social standing, and even gender, to tell us we are all equal when it comes to the promises of God and being part of Abraham's family. Not only are we a part of the family, but we are heirs, receiving the family inheritances like all the other kids in the family of God. What a fabulous plan! The exciting part is the emphasis on *the now*. It was not just for people in past history. It's for people like you and me who are living in the 21st century. We *are* heirs—present tense! This news and possibility is as current as today's news.

What a promise! The promise of freedom from any past or present curses through the impartation of the blessing of God to Abraham is yours today, by an act of faith. You are privileged; you now have the Word of God to act upon and to use to declare your freedom from past bondages! I remind you that we are not dealing with some kind of fanciful theory, but reality that works because God's Word and promises are infallible. This is eternal truth for today and every day.

———•———

Here's how it worked in the life of Bridget, a young lady who was 35 years old. She was diagnosed by her doctor as being grossly obese. She had attempted just about every diet possible but with no lasting results. So the doctor suggested the possibility of a gastric by-pass surgery. But there was the danger of complications to be considered if she were to proceed. It was a tough choice.

Her lonely nights were spent in regretting the last snack she had just consumed. She'd stand in front of her mirror and condemn herself. She was trapped and cursed by her weight problem.

Her plight came to a pastor's attention because of Bridget's mother. In her frustration, Bridget's mother went to her pastor and said, "Bridget has a real problem. She and I have tried everything we know how to do. Would you mind talking to her? She lives out of town and an appointment needs to be made ahead of time so she can schedule for it."

The pastor replied, "I'm not a weight specialist ... but sure, I'll talk to her." And the appointment was set.

Bridget arrived at the appointed time and indicated she really wanted a solution. She talked out some of her frustrations as the pastor listened.

He replied, "Let's get right to the issue. You are speaking curses on yourself with your negative self-talk. You stand in front of your mirror and tell yourself you are ugly and fat. When you do this, you don't see the beautiful young lady you can become. Are you ready to let God help you to do it His way?"

She looked at him and agreed. "But how can God help me with my weight problem?" she asked.

"It's really quite easy. Let's begin with the Word of God. Does it declare you are fat and ugly?"

"Well ... no."

"What does the Word of God have to say about you and your curse?"

"Okay, I get your point."

"Tell you what ... you go home and begin a Bible study about how you can break your curse, and come back and see me in a week," the pastor said and gave her an assignment of specific scriptures to read.

The week passed and Bridget returned with a smile on her face. "I'm already doing better. I have decided to apply these Bible verses to myself every day just like I take my medical prescriptions." The pastor encouraged her before she left.

Because she lived in another city, the pastor didn't see her for many, many months. One particular Sunday, as the pastor stood greeting folks following the Sunday service, he felt a tug on his coat sleeve and turned to see Bridget with her hand behind her head doing a pirouette like a model. "How do you like the new me?" she asked. Then without hardly pausing to take a breath, she continued, "I have lost one hundred and forty-seven pounds!"

Then she gave the pastor a hug, and together they celebrated how the power and promises of God had worked in her life! What an example of how the power of the blessing defeats the power of a curse!

———•———

TO GIVE US A GREATER UNDERSTANDING of the blessing, let's take a deeper look at its meaning. The word "bless" derives its meaning from words in both the Old and New Testament. The former comes from the Hebrew *barak,* and the later comes from the Greek *eulogeo.* Both have the meaning "speak a blessing." God performed this act over His creation in Genesis 1:22, "God blessed them . . . ." What did He bless? The critters that lived in the waters and the ones who flew in the air. Then in verse 27, "Male and female He created them. God blessed them . . . ." He blessed His creations—human and animal.

The word *barak* means to convey a gift with a powerful utterance. *Eulogeo* is the foundation of our word "eulogy," meaning to speak well of, to cause benefit, to make happy and prosperous as well as to include welfare, happiness and protection.

When blessings are spoken, it releases God's power, goodness, favor, and protection. When God spoke His blessings, He released His power and purpose over the future of those being blessed.

A blessing when spoken, written, or read is anticipating a productive future!

Study Guide

How does God's blessing work in my life, in my situation? Start by reading Deuteronomy 23:5 once more.

1. What is this promise saying to you, right now?

_____

_____

_____

2. Describe some of the ways in which God loves you.

_____

_____

_____

3. From the New Testament, read Galatians 3:6-14, 26-29.

_____

_____

_____

4. Why do you think this has become the most important promise in regard to the blessing?

_____

_____

_____

5. How will you apply these promises to your life?

_____

_____

_____

God planned for life to be imparted to His people through the spoken blessing.

The Old Testament fathers expected the blessing to release God's favor into their lives and the lives of their families!

That same expectation can rest in the hearts of all who accept the challenge to learn the biblical way to bless.

—*William T. Ligon, Sr., Author/Professor*

Chapter Five

Choose a Different Ancestor

A very happy mother shared the following testimonial with me. "I never realized how important or how powerful the blessing can be until I read your book, *The B Word* (published by Evergreen Press). We have one very hyperactive son. He's been on Ritalin and other drugs which haven't really helped. Then we began speaking blessings over this boy, and we began to see marked improvement. Every day we bless him with peace, joy, self-control, a good attitude, favor with his teachers, and to have an unselfish love for others and the Lord. What an improvement! Thank you."

We need to understand the two different kinds of curses mentioned in the New Testament. Both of these have an impact on our living. The first is "the curse of the law" or better understood as the original curse of sin.

> *All who rely on observing the law are under a curse . . . clearly no one is justified before God by the law* (Galatians 3:10).

This curse was broken with the death and resurrection of Jesus Christ.

> *Christ redeemed us from the curse of the law by becoming a curse for us* (Galatians 3:13).

He released us from the consequences of sin. "For the wages of sin is death" (Romans 6:23). All of us who have become believers—Christians—can and do rejoice in the fact that the blessing of Abraham has broken the curse of sin over us. It happens every time a sinner turns and accepts Jesus Christ as Lord and Savior. Paul also declares that this is a blessing:

> *David says the same thing when he speaks of the blessedness of the person (man) to whom God credits righteousness apart from works: "Blessed are they whose transgressions are forgiven, who sins are covered. Blessed is the person (man) whose sin the Lord will never count against them"* (Romans 4:6-8).

This is the central message of the Bible and has been quite well preached and taught by the church.

Consider with me the second type of curse. We can call this a "malediction," which is a spoken curse or an action modeled by another person, and could also be seen as a curse. The power of this kind of curse is noted by God when He said,

I will bless those who bless you, and whoever curses you I will curse (Genesis 12:3).

The bitterness of this kind of a curse is illustrated in the book of James, written by the brother of Jesus:

Out of the same mouth proceedeth blessing and cursing. My brethren, these things ought not so to be. Doth a fountain send forth at the same place sweet water and bitter? (James 3:10-11, KJV)

Sad to say, for the most part the church has neglected this biblical teaching about the power of the blessing to break the power of this kind of curse. Paul highlights the difference and the power of the blessing over the curse when he wrote,

Bless those who persecute you; bless and do not curse (Romans 12:10).

This verse demonstrates how the blessing is greater and more powerful than the curse. Jesus also emphasized this power when He commanded:

But I tell you who hear me: Love your enemies, do good to those who hate you, bless those

who curse you, pray for those who mistreat you (Luke 6:27-28).

It's pretty clear ... the power of the blessing is more powerful and overcomes the power of the malediction kind of curse. You make the choice: Good is always more powerful than evil!

One of the church fathers, Augustine, in the third century compared good and evil to light and darkness. Darkness is the absence of light. Therefore evil is the absence of good. Nobody ever turned on the darkness. But we can turn on the light! Darkness and evil come when the light is removed. The power of the blessing is one way to turn on the light.

We're talking again about choice. You have the power and ability to make a powerful choice when confronting a family curse. It happened in the life choice of an eight-year-old prince who became a king.

———————

Manasseh was the grandfather, and he became a king at twelve years of age but his reign was a total disaster. He led his nation back into idol worship and destroyed the Israelites' places of worship. He led the people in the practices of witchcraft, divination, and human sacrifice. When he died we are introduced to the next generation.

Manasseh was twelve years old when he became king, and he reigned in Jerusalem fifty-five years. His mother's name was Hephzibah. He did evil in the eyes of the Lord, following the detestable practices of the nations the Lord had driven out before the Israelites. He rebuilt the high places his father Hezekiah had destroyed; he also erected altars to Baal and made an Asherah pole, as Ahab king of Israel had done. He bowed down to all the starry hosts and worshipped them (2 Kings 21:1-3).

Amon was the father, and he became a king at twenty-two years of age. He was equally as vile as his father. His reign was another unmitigated disaster, and it was cut short by a palace conspiracy. He was assassinated, and the next king came on the scene.

Amon was twenty-two years old when he became king, and he reigned in Jerusalem two years. His mother's name was Meshullemeth daughter of Harus; she was from Jotbah. He did evil in the eyes of the Lord, as his father Manasseh had done. He walked in all the ways of his father; he worshiped the idols his father had worshiped and bowed down to them. He forsook the Lord, the God of his fathers, and did not walk in the way of the Lord (2 Kings 21:19-22).

Josiah was Amon's son. He was only eight years old when he was anointed king! He reigned for thirty-one years, and those three decades were some of the happiest in the nation's history. What was the key? The Bible says he did what was right. Let's read it:

> *He (Josiah) did what was right in the eyes of the Lord and walked in all the ways of his father David, not turning aside to the right or left* (II Kings 22:2).

Whoa! Wait a minute. Did we miss something? David was not his physical, biological father. Josiah didn't follow the ways of his grandfather, King Manasseh, nor in the footsteps of his physical father, King Amon. He walked in the ways of his spiritual father, David! How did this happen and why?

Josiah made a quality decision. When his father was murdered, Josiah inherited the throne in Judah, yes, but he also received all the baggage that went with it. He and his nation were under the curse of the past: two generations who were cursed by the choices their leadership had made. He could have continued to live under that curse or remove the curse.

He went back in history and stopped with King David—a king who was not perfect, but a man who, at the core of his being, was a man after God's own heart. He was seen as the apple of God's eye. In this choice, Josiah changed his future and the future of the people for whom he was responsible.

He chose well. He chose a new mentor, a new example to follow—a new father. He leaped over two unworthy generations to pick a winner! With this choice Josiah reversed the curse that had been his and he lived out his days in the blessings provided through his forefather David. It changed his life! It changed the future of his nation! (Read the entire story in II Kings 21 and 22.)

————◆————

IS THERE A LIFE PRIN-CIPLE we can learn here? Yes! If Josiah did it and it worked, then you and I can make such a choice and reverse the flow of the negative from the past and turn it into the blessing of the present and future.

Turn the curse into a blessing to fashion an entirely new history for your generation.

You may be thinking, *But I don't have any worthy ancestors, what then?* There's an easy answer. You have a loving heavenly Father, and His only Son, who are the family members you need to be your mentors. Josiah leaped over two previous generations and changed the curse into a blessing. Reverse the flow. Turn the curse into a blessing to be an entirely new history for your generation and the generations to follow.

The promises in regards to the blessing all have long tails. I remind you of this ancient promise,

I, the Lord your God, am a jealous God, punishing the children for the sin of the fathers to the third and fourth generation of those who hate me, but showing LOVE TO A THOUSAND GENERATIONS OF THOSE WHO LOVE ME and keep my commandments (Exodus 20:5-6).

Evil has a limited curse to the third or fourth generation. But to people who love their God, the blessing can be extended to a thousand generations! Remember: God's love reverses the curse!

———•———

Patricia approached me at the close of a service in which this message of freedom had just been preached. She was in her early sixties. Tears streamed down her face, and she asked, "May I speak with you a moment?"

I replied, "Sure."

She went on, "Today, for the very first time in my life, I have been set free!" She was laughing, smiling, and crying, all at the same time.

She continued, "Here's some of my story. When my mother passed away some years ago, my father remarried. Today, my father has also been gone about four years. His second wife, my stepmother, was an angry, money-grubbing, controlling witch who was impossible to get along with! But that's not all. When my father passed away, his entire estate—and it was sizable—was passed to his new wife. Then, she died. All of my father's estate that should have gone to my brother and me was willed to her family. My father left us absolutely nothing. Nothing! Not even a blessing. Not even his Bible. Nothing to remember him by other than memories."

She paused to catch her breath and brush away her tears. Then she went on, "I have been bitter and angry for years. My life is miserable, my husband and kids are miserable, all because of me. My health is bad. I'm sick with diabetes, arthritis, and obesity. But today, for the first time, I understand that God is my loving Father! He is the source and the giver of the blessing! Today, I know He has broken the curse of bitterness I was passing on to my own kids. I've been set free. The power of this curse over me is broken! I now receive the blessing, and I plan to live the rest of my days under his blessings!"

Together, we celebrated her victory. Then, after a number of months had passed, she reported that her diabetes was under control, her arthritis was no longer bothering her, and she lost more than 160 pounds! She reported to being a new person, all because of the power of the blessing to overcome the curse.

Study Guide

1. Perhaps this is a new concept to you. If it is, what is your thinking, now?

_____

_____

_____

2. How do you think you can put this principle to work for you?

_____

_____

_____

3. Who might your ancestors be, whom you need to leap over when thinking of your future?

_____

_____

_____

4. Why do you think this is such a powerful insight?

_____

_____

_____

5. Describe how you will let go of the past and move into a blessed future.

_____

_____

_____

When we bless, something living and active is released in the invisible world around us that brings positive benefits.

—*M. Lynn Reddick, Ph.D., Author/Professor*

Chapter Six

The Implications of the Blessing
of Abraham in Your Life

The Gibson family lived near us as I was growing up. They had only one child, Lyle, who acted like a spoiled brat all the time. As neighbors my brother and I played together with him and other neighborhood kids. The Gibsons were people who went to church on a regular basis and were quite strict in raising their son. But all of us kids overheard lots of family "discussions" from the Gibson family because they were loud, and they didn't seem to care who heard them.

Never did I hear them praise Lyle for anything he

had done. Never did they bless him. Never was there a word of encouragement. It was always, "Lyle, you klutz, if you don't behave you will end up in jail. Lyle, if you don't get better grades, we'll send you to reform school. Lyle, keep on doing what you're doing and you'll be a failure in life..." and much more along the same line. He grew up as a very needy kid.

And sure enough, their warnings and predictions came true! Lyle was a failure in life when measured against any kind of success standards and eventually did wind up in prison doing hard time. He lived his life under the curse placed upon him by his parents. All their predictions were self-fulfilling prophecies.

———•———

WORDS CAN CUT! One Hebrew word from the Old Testament is *qabab*, which means to "execute or stab another person with words." Words can be as lethal as a stab wound! Another word is *naqab*, meaning to "to punch something hard enough to perforate the object."

There is power in the words that we speak.

Words can cut to the quick of a person's soul. They can be thrown hard enough and often enough to punch holes in the spirit and being of another person who becomes the object of such violence. There is power in the words that we speak. The Bible tells us we have the power to bless or curse—we can do one or the other, but not both.

Jesus related to people on the basis of what they could become. For example, while they were beginners, untrained and ignorant, he told them they were "the salt of the earth" and "the light of the world." He saw future potential and spoke blessings on them as if it were a reality.

Both Isaac and Jacob related to their sons on the same basis when they blessed them. "By faith Isaac blessed Jacob and Esau in regard to the future. By faith Jacob, when he was dying, blessed each of Joseph's sons" (Hebrews 11:20-21). Jacob also blessed each of his twelve sons and pictured exciting and fulfilling futures for them. We find that example in Genesis chapter forty-nine.

Today when we think of future potential in those whom we may bless and in our own life as we appropriate the blessings laid up for us, the future promises to be fantastic. The potential of the blessing is enormous. Here is the biblical promise,

> *He* [Christ] *redeemed us in order that the blessing given* [by God] *to Abraham might come to the Gentiles* [that's us] *through Christ Jesus* (Galatians 3:14).

Let's be specific. Just what are the blessings and benefits given to Abraham, which, according to the Bible, are now ours because of the sacrifice of Christ? Let's take some time to examine the seven-part blessing given to Abraham. Understand that this blessing is the basis of God's care for the Jewish people and nation. It's really foundational to all of God's workings in the world. But there is also a personal application for you and me! There is one way to understand the meaning, but there are any number of applications that can be made. This foundational blessing is found in Genesis 12:2-3.

> *I will make you into a great nation and I will bless you; I will make your name great, and you will be a blessing.*
>
> *I will bless those who bless you, and whoever curses you I will curse; and all peoples on earth will be blessed through you.*

There are seven distinct promises of blessing expressed here.

1. **I [God] will make you into a great nation.**

Abraham and Sarah were one couple, now up in age, and with no children—no heirs through which this great nation would be built. But we know the story. Out of this tiny beginning, God did build a great nation—a nation still in existence today against all odds. Satan, through the ages and down to our present day, has done everything in his power to destroy the Jewish people, but God's promise is still in effect!

Let's take the time to look at a current illustration of the effect of this promise. Since the Nobel Prize has come into existence and been awarded, the Muslims, who also claim Abraham as their progenitor and number some 1,200,000,000 people—equal to about 20% of the world's population—have been awarded 8 Nobel Prizes. These included one for peace for Yasser Arafat, and another to Albert Camus. Camus was actually born a Frenchman, but raised as a Muslim in North Africa, and he was awarded the prize for literature.

In contrast, the Jews who number approximately 14,000,000, about 0.02% of the world's population have been awarded 10 in literature; 8 in peace; 22 in chemistry; 14 in economics; 45 in medicine; and 31 in physics. That's a total of 129 Nobel Prizes! Think of how they have blessed the world. Though they are small in number, they are great in achievements. I attribute this accomplishment to the promise God gave Abraham! There are any number of ways in which to become a great nation.

What does this promise mean to you and yours? If you are a believer, in the same way that Abraham was a believer, you can, by faith, claim these same physical, spiritual, natural, and future blessings upon you and your family. It means this promise of God can and will add value to you and your family. I remind you that the blessing in Abraham's life allowed him to be something that would have been impossible without this blessing.

Here's the promise to help you stake your claim to this blessing:

> *The Lord your God is GOD; He is the faithful God, keeping his blessings (covenant) of love to a thousand generations of those who love Him and keep His commandments* (Deut. 7:9).

2. And I will bless you.

God said, "I will bless you!" Think of the awesome possibilities. It means exactly what it says! Blessing in what ways? In every way. I see no limits to this promise. I will bless you! Incredible! In spite of persecutions, wars, uprisings, rebellions, Communism, and the Holocaust, we can see the Jewish people tend to rise to the top, like cream, in many ways. No matter what happens, the Jews seem to be able to prosper. This has been another blessing with long tails.

Take the current financial situation in the resurrected nation of Israel. The nation has risen out of nothing in 1948 to its current strong condition. In spite of having only 7 million people living in Israel, it is now home to more than 6,600 millionaires! Today Israel has become an economic powerhouse, one of the world's high-tech leaders, and a magnet for foreign investment. "Israel is like part of Silicon Valley," according to Microsoft founder Bill Gates. "And," he continued, "the quality of people here is fantastic!"

According to Joel Rosenberg in *Epicenter*, "there are more Israeli-based companies and companies started by Israelis listed on NASDAQ than from any other country."

Benjamin Netanyahu, in a speech delivered in June 2005, predicted, "In ten years, Israel could be one of the ten richest countries in the world!"

Understand that I'm not talking about a "prosperity gospel." God has not promised to make you super rich or the winner of a lottery. Note that in the Bible you might also be promised persecution, trials, temptations, troubles, and maybe even martyrdom.

But the promise to bless means God is at work adding value to your life and living. The added value may be as simple as a 3% unexpected raise, an extra hundred thousand trouble-free miles on your ten-year-old car, years without medical expense, years with no financial emergencies, and on and on. Of course we still need to pray, "Give us our daily bread." Food on your table may be the blessing.

The implications of this blessing are enormous! Maybe we need to pray, "Lord, open my eyes so I can see the blessings You are providing in my life!" There are little blessings and big blessings ... blessings we become aware of and blessings that are showered down of which we are unaware ... blessings we recognize and blessings we don't. There are blessings of added value that go unnoticed.

King Agur caught this sense of balance in life in his prayer:

> *Two things I ask of you, O Lord; do not refuse me before I die: Keep falsehood and lies far from me; give me neither poverty nor riches, but give me only my daily bread. Otherwise, I may have too much and disown you and say, 'Who is the Lord?' Or I may become poor and steal, and so dishonor the name of my God* (Proverbs 30:7-9).

3. I will make your name great.

God has more than fulfilled this promise. Abraham is one of the most recognized names in the world! He is the father of all we hold dear in the spiritual realm. To the Jew, he is father of their nation. To the Arabic nations, he is considered their father as well. Without Abraham and the Jewish people, there would be no Bible, no knowledge of God, no Christianity, and no church.

When we think of the term "great" think of the big picture. Great can mean any or all of the following:

vast, immense, huge, large, big, colossal, stupendous, prodigious, outstanding, notable, prominent, significant, important, strong, momentous, leading, famous, noted, renowned, eminent, celebrated, distinguished, esteemed, terrific, excellent and more! Wow!

I pray, Lord, help me to be like the blessed man of Psalms 1:1-2,

> Blessed is the man who does not walk in the counsel of the wicked or stand in the way of sinners or sit in the seat of mockers. But his delight is in the law of the Lord, and on his law he meditates day and night!

May God help all of us to live our lives in such a way as to please and bless our heavenly Father, and then leave the greatness of our name up to Him.

4. And you will be a blessing.

This is the fourth statement of the seven-part blessing. Here is a turning of the focus. It's a turn from being on the receiving end to being a giver. This is the point at which this blessing thing really takes on wings and changes the world around us.

Without Abraham and his nation there would be no recorded word of God. No Bible. No prophets. (I know, God could have followed "plan B" if needed.) But with Abraham being the first and best choice to be a blessing, the plan of God for the ages is still in effect and moving toward a final wrap-up of human history. Can you begin to imagine what this world would be like without the blessing of Abraham?

Notice the tense in which this blessing was given— the future tense. "You *will be ...*" You don't even have to sing, "Make me a blessing..." because when you are part of the family of Abraham, *you will be* a blessing! Jesus promised and blessed his followers,

"You are the *light of the world*." Light dispels the darkness, light replaces darkness, light shows the way, and light is attractive to people who are in the dark.

"You are the *salt of the world!*" Salt is the seasoning of life; salt makes lots of things palatable. Salt improves the lifestyle. Salt along with iodine helps keep the body healthy, but salt that is not salty is thrown out. As we bless, we are the salt of the world— seasoning it, changing it, making it a better place.

"You are a *city on a hilltop*." You can become a place of refuge to the hurting, a place for them to run to for protection, a place of comfort, a place to get away from the cold and darkness of this world.

As we receive the blessing of Abraham, you and I will rise to the level of the blessings of Jesus Christ. We have a purpose in life. We are destined to be something special. It's called "being a blessing." Our constant prayer should be: "Lord, I begin the day with you. You have blessed me. Now help me to be a blessing to at least one person I meet today." As this begins to happen in your life, please be sure to give Him the glory for the results of the blessing in the life of another person.

5. I will bless those who bless you.

What a promise! What a wonderful, comforting blessing, and it's still in effect today. It's amazing—here are blessings for those who bless Israel. It's really quite simple. People who are leaders of our nation and other nations of the world need to understand how this works. It's a matter of sowing and reaping on a national scale.

Americans, look around. Notice how God has kept His promise. Our nation has honored and protected Israel, and I believe this promise is directly connected to our nation's prosperity. Like you, I too want this blessing on America to continue.

The Jewish people among us who have migrated to our shores have brought a unique blessing to us. Think of the Jews who have blessed us with material and financial prosperity, scientific breakthroughs, excellence in literature, artistic renown, architectural advances, medical discoveries, nuclear power, and men on the moon. And there are many more ways that the blessing has come back to us. America has helped the underprivileged and refugees of the world, especially in our care of the Jews, and it's had a fabulous return!

Individually we can also trigger this return of a blessing. It still works. When we bless the Jewish people, God will bless us in return. How? We can begin by praying for the peace of Jerusalem. We can be part of ministry to them. We can talk to our leaders about the need for peace in Jerusalem. Be creative. There are still ways to bless this nation.

There's a fascinating nugget of truth from the life of Jacob and that rascally scoundrel, Laban, father-in-law to Jacob. I remind you that Laban is the man who tricked an unsuspecting Jacob on his wedding night by switching brides—the older sister in place of Rachel. Read the story again. What an all-time family battle takes place! The nugget is found recorded in Genesis 30:27 (NKJ),

> *Laban said to him, "Please stay if I have found favor in your eyes, for I have learned by experience that the Lord has blessed me for your sake."*

It's incredible. Even a nasty character like Laban recognized the blessing he received because of God's blessing on Jacob. Let's live in the blessing of God in such a way that even our boss or employer is blessed because of us!

On a more personal level, as we bless others, God will in turn bless us. Jesus said:

> *Do not judge, and you will not be judged. Do not condemn, and you will not be condemned.*

Forgive, and you will be forgiven. Give and it will be given to you (Luke 6:37-38).

But the return comes back in greater measure than what we have given. There's a spiritual law here that works when it's triggered. Our act of giving sets wonderful things into motion. Here's how the blessing returns according to Jesus, but don't forget the caveat at the end.

Give, and it will be given to you. A good measure, pressed down, shaken together and running over will be poured into your lap For with the measure you use, it will be measured to you (v. 38).

Jesus puts the cap on this concept, "...remembering the words the Lord Jesus himself said: 'It is more blessed to give than to receive'" (Acts 20:35). It's easy to say, but not as easy to do or to understand.

Also, if and when people honor, respect, and bless you, make sure you give honor and glory and praise to God for His blessings through another. After all, it's His plan, and He still makes it work!

6. And whoever curses you I will curse.

This is breathtaking when you consider the scope of this part of the Abrahamic blessing. The protection of the progeny of Abraham can easily be traced through history. Whoever has persecuted or cursed these people has suffered consequences. We can easily name off some of the leaders who have come under the curse of God because of their mistreatment of the people of Israel. Begin with Pharaoh, who drowned in the Red Sea after being the recipient of the plagues concluding with the death of his and other firstborn sons in Egypt. We can continue with Goliath, Jezebel, and Nebuchadnezzar from ancient history. Does it still hold true in modern times? Continue the listing with such characters as Josef Stalin, Adolph Hitler, Saddam Hussein, Osama bin Laden, Achmadinijad, Yasser Arafat, and others. God promised and delivered on a promise with this blessing, and it's been fulfilled.

Abraham received personal protection many times. At least twice when kings had designs on his wife, Abraham was protected from himself and his half lies. When he went into battle with his personal army, he was victorious. And if God ever pulls the curtain back and gives us a deeper look at his life, we can just imagine how many more times God's protection was around him without Abraham being aware of it.

This truth is exhibited elsewhere in the life of the nation of Israel. A most notable occasion was when the Ammonites and Moabites attempted to place a curse on the nation of Israel. Well, let's read a bit of that account from Deuteronomy 23:4-5:

They (the Ammonites and Moabites) hired

> *Balaam* [a sorcerer] ... *to pronounce a curse*
> *on you (the Israelites). HOWEVER, the Lord*
> *your God would not listen to Balaam BUT*
> *turned the curse into a BLESSING for YOU,*
> *because the Lord your God LOVES YOU!*

If God did it for Israel, what do you think He will do on your behalf? If God did it once, why can't He do it again? Do you think God loved the Israelites any more than He loves you and me, particularly at times when we may have been cursed?

What does this mean for twenty-first century people? The Bible predicted we would be living in perilous times, and sure enough, we are. We can appropriate this part of the blessing as Abraham did—by faith.

7. **And all peoples on earth will be blessed through you.**

This is the final of the seven promises and may well be the most beneficial to our world. It's awesome to be able to bless the world! How? This, of course, is a prophetic promise regarding the coming Messiah, Jesus Christ. Because of His first coming, the whole world has the possibility of becoming part of the family of God. "John (the Baptist) saw Jesus coming toward him and said, 'Look, the Lamb of God, who takes away the sin of the world'" (John 1:29).

Paul the Apostle gives us clarification about this particular part of the blessing of Abraham:

> *Consider Abraham: "He believed God, and it was credited to him as righteousness." Understand, then, that those who believe are children of Abraham. The Scripture foresaw that God would justify the Gentiles by faith, and announced the gospel in advance to Abraham: "All nations will be blessed through you." So those who have faith are blessed along with Abraham, the man of faith* (Galatians 3:6-9).

Abraham was a man of faith to such an extent that God entrusted to him the plan of the ages—how the world would be saved hundreds of years later with the birth, life, death, and resurrection of Jesus Christ!

The implications for us are plain. When you share this gospel with another person, you are blessing the world! It happens when you become a prayer intercessor for others to become Christians; when your lifestyle blesses others; when you support ministries with your finances; when you do a hands-on-mission trip in America or beyond.

Now comes a really big question. Does this blessing thing really work or is it more pie-in-the-sky empty promises? The Bible is the best commentary on itself. So once more, we go back into the Word of God to answer the question!

Abraham was now old and well advanced in years, and the Lord had blessed him in every way (Genesis 24:1)

"In every way." It sounds to me like that is pretty inclusive! You name the "every way," and God did it: body, mind, soul, spirit—yes, and a whole lot more! Every way!

Did this blessing spill over onto anybody else? How about his wife, Sarah? Well into her old age, she was childless and unable to become pregnant with the son through whom a nation would also be born. Let's read the account:

God said to Abraham, "As for Sarai your wife, you are no longer to call her Sarai; her name will be Sarah. I will bless her And will surely give you a son by her!" (Genesis 17:15-16)

Notice that God didn't say, "I will *heal* her," and she shall have a son. No! God said, "I will *bless* her!" There's a difference. Isn't a healing a type of blessing? Yes! But a blessing is much more complete. A by-product of the blessing happened to be a change that allowed her to bear a son at the age of ninety and receive much more, as well as a life filled with joy! You, like Sarah, may not need a healing as much as you need the blessing of God!

Well, what about that son—did he benefit because of the blessing in his father's life? In other words,

could the blessing be passed on to the next generation? That's also part of the family record:

> *Abraham left everything he owned to Isaac*
> *(Genesis 25:5).*

Did that include the passing of the blessing to his
son? It says "everything" therefore it must mean
everything. What proof do we have that the blessing
was included? Again, we have it recorded:

> *After Abraham's death, God blessed his son*
> *Isaac (Genesis 25:11).*

So how do we know if the blessing was still active
and effective and would produce the same results in
this generation? Let's read on. A disaster is about to
overtake the land where Isaac lives. This is the very
same dilemma his father faced when he abandoned the
land because of famine and went down to Egypt. This
is the test of the blessing:

> *The Lord appeared to Isaac and said, "Do not*
> *go down to Egypt; live in the land where I tell*
> *you to live. Stay in this land ... I will be with*
> *you and will bless you" (Genesis 26:2-3).*

So Isaac obeyed this directive and stayed. What
happened then?

> *So King Abimelech gave orders to all the*
> *people: "Anyone who molests the man or his*
> *wife shall surely be put to death!" (Genesis*
> *26:11)*

There it is—plain for all of us to see—divine protection at work. The king recognized something special in Isaac's life. But the blessing was more than protection. There's another huge benefit of the blessing:

> *Isaac planted crops in that land and the same year reaped a hundredfold, because the Lord had blessed him* (Genesis 26:13).

The blessing passed on from Abraham to Isaac and became a reality in the form of divine protection. It also could be counted in hard cash with a bumper crop in the middle of a famine. What did the neighbors think? They had very little crop while the blessed one, Isaac, had a hundredfold crop! That's another instance of the blessing at work in the life of a human being.

Is it possible that a blessing could be given to a prospective member of this family? What about the wife whom Isaac was to marry? Could she also be a person to receive a blessing? She, Rebecca, was about to leave her home and family and, as a farewell, a blessing is pronounced on her future. Her family pronounced this blessing:

> *So they sent their sister Rebecca on her way ... And they blessed Rebecca and said to her: "Our sister, may you increase to thousands upon thousands; may your offspring possess the gates of their enemies"* (Genesis 24:59-60).

And it goes on. Will the blessing still be effective on

the next generation in the lives of the grandchildren? Isaac and Rebecca had two sons, twins, and what a story that turned out to be. But our question hasn't been answered. Is the blessing still alive in grandsons?

Jacob, you recall, ran away after he had stolen the first blessing, the blessing reserved for the oldest. He fled to his mother's uncle, Laban, who was a scoundrel if there ever was a scoundrel. To make the story short, the blessing on Jacob's life was evident, until he was forced to leave with his wives and his flocks and herds. Here's the point of the story:

> *Then God came to Laban ... in a dream and said to him: "Be careful not to say anything to Jacob, either good or bad!"* (Genesis 31:24)

That's another example of divine protection because of the blessing being in force. The blessing was so powerful in Jacob's messed-up life that the old scoundrel, Laban, was blessed because of Jacob.

The blessing can help someone else because it's on your life. Think of the blessing to a boss, to an employer, to a neighbor, to your family, to your extended family, to the next—and more—generations! It's incredible!

All of this and the power of the blessing to break family or generational curses in your life!

Study Guide

1. How does the blessing of Abraham help us today?

_____

_____

_____

2. How can the seven-part blessing of Abraham help you break a family curse?

_____

_____

_____

3. Which of these aspects of the blessing are the most important to you?

_____

_____

_____

Why?

_____

_____

4. Name the ways in which you can pass along these benefits to another person.

_____

_____

_____

5. Name some of the ways in which God's blessing impacted the life of Abraham.

_____

_____

_____

6. Name the ways it can impact your life.

_____

_____

_____

7. How will this blessing bring added value to your life?

_____

_____

_____

The good Samaritan was blessed!

How do I know?

Because he blessed others.

He was so confident of his relationship to God that he could overlook prejudice, fear, and doubt to become practically and lovingly involved in blessing those around him!

—*H. Norman Wright, Counselor/Author*

Chapter Seven

Now It's Your Turn

Okay. So you've been blessed and the power of the blessing has broken the curses of the past. You've been set free from the bondage of a family curse. Now what? It's your responsibility to share this power of blessing with someone else. The blessings of God are not to be hoarded but to be shared. When you share and bless others, the blessings in and on your life can only increase. The more you give, the more you receive.

This is a principle contrary to the way of thinking in the world where to increase your holdings you keep them and nurture them. But in the spiritual realm, it works in the opposite way. Give and it will be given unto you! It's time to increase the value of somebody else! Bless and you will be blessed!

There are some principles at work when considering God's blessings in your life. 1) God desires and wants to bless people. 2) God uses people such as you and me to bless others. 3) When God's people have been blessed, there is an expectation for us to bless others. 4) There is a pattern God has provided when blessing others. 5) Those who are blessed experience an added value in their life, and the blessers also experience improved lives.

As we have already discovered in past chapters, the blessings of God can be passed on, especially to the next generation. Biblically the pattern of blessing was demonstrated by:

- Fathers passing it on to children.

- Grandparents blessed grandchildren,

- Simeon blessed the infant Jesus and His parents,

- Jesus blessed little children,

- Jesus blessed His followers in many ways and concluded His earthly ministry by a final blessing,

- The early church apostles blessed the church,

- Leaders blessed followers,

- Church leaders blessed their congregations,

• And the people blessed the Lord God of heaven!

It's simple in principle. Delegated authorities are all of God's people. In the Old Testament the specific responsibility was upon family members. Then, when the ministry of the Tabernacle was outlined by God, it fell to the Levites to speak the blessings. In our era, the priesthood is made up of all believers. And the responsibility to bless is ours, according to the Apostle Peter (I Peter 2:9-10).

But you are a chosen people, a royal priesthood, a holy nation, a people belonging to God, that you may declare the praises of him who called you out of darkness into his wonderful light.

Once you were not a people, but now you are the people of God; once you had not received mercy, but now you have received mercy.

How do we bless others? The overwhelming biblical method was to give others a spoken blessing. Paul the Apostle wrote blessings as part of his closing statement in many of his letters, which are now the epistles we read.

Beyond speaking the blessing, in many of the recorded blessings in Scripture, there was a "laying on of hands" or another meaningful touch that accompanied the giving of the blessing.

For example, when sharing a blessing with another,

you might place a hand on a shoulder or take someone by the hand and speak your blessing.

What should be said? Make sure it's a message that depicts a positive, uplifting future. Think it over carefully. What would you like to see happen in the future in the life of the person you are blessing?

Make sure the message is one that places a high value on the person whom you are blessing. Remember that God loves all people and desires that each experience added value as well as a reminder of His presence.

Along with the spoken message, be prepared to also participate in that person's life to help the blessing be fulfilled. Do you care enough to share in a person's future?

Always keep in mind that God is in the business of adding value to our lives in many kinds of ways—not only financially. Of course it can come in the form of money, but there are many things of more value than money.

It's also exciting when you can bless others with the Word of God. Place their names inside of a biblical blessing. An excellent example of a biblical blessing is found in Psalm 128:1-6,

> *Blessed are all who fear the Lord, Who walk in his ways.*

- *You will eat the fruit of your labor; blessings and prosperity will be yours.*

- *Your wife will be like a fruitful vine within your house;*

- *Your sons will be like olive shoots around your table.*

Thus is the man blessed who fears the Lord.

- *May the Lord bless you from Zion all the days of your life;*

- *May you see the prosperity of Jerusalem,*

- *And may you live to see your children's children.*

- *Peace be upon Israel!*

Wonderful! Anyone and everyone can be a blessing to someone else! It makes no difference if you are young or old, immature in the faith or mature, or how busy you are, how skilled or unskilled, how articulate or inarticulate—you can bless others! But especially if you have been blessed, you, above all others, should bless!

Extending a Blessing

Here's a simple definition of extending a blessing to another person:

A blessing begins with a meaningful touch. It continues with a spoken, thoughtful message of high value—a message that pictures a special future for the person you are blessing. This message is also based on an active commitment to see the blessing come to pass as much as possible.

Here's another way to look at the five basic parts of the blessing:

1. A meaningful touch.

2. A positive spoken message.

3. Attaching "high value" to the person being blessed.

4. Picturing, by faith, a special future for the one being blessed.

5. An active commitment to help fulfill the blessing being given.

It's your turn. Be creative! Use these words and this book as seed thoughts to help you bless others. There are many ways to pass along this powerful life-changer!

———◆———

The Sneeze!

They walked in tandem, each of the ninety-two students filing into the already crowded auditorium.

With their rich maroon gowns flowing and traditional caps with tassels, they looked almost as grown up as they felt.

Fathers swallowed hard behind proud, broad smiles, and mothers freely wiped away tears of joy.

But this class of graduates would *not* pray during this commencement—not by their choice, but because of a recent court ruling prohibiting it.

The school president, several speakers and students were careful to stay within the guidelines allowed by this ruling. Inspirational and challenging speeches were delivered, but no one mentioned divine guidance, and no one invoked blessings on the graduates, nor on their families. The speeches were nice and routine, until the final speech, which received a standing ovation!

A solitary student walked proudly to the podium and stood silent at the microphone for a moment or two. Then ... it happened! All ninety-two graduates, yes, every single one, on cue, simultaneously loudly sneezed!

The student on stage simply paused, looked at the audience and the graduates and said, "God bless you— each and every one of you!"

And he walked off the stage as the audience jumped to its feet and exploded into long and loud applause! This class of graduates had found a unique way to invoke God's blessing on their future with or without the court's approval!

What a great little story. It supposedly happened at the mid-year graduation at the University of Maryland.

All together now, we can all find a way to say it and do it. GOD BLESS YOU!

Now it's your turn to pass on the blessing to another person!

Study Guide

1. When you are blessed, what are the implications for you?

_____

_____

_____

2. When you bless others, what are the benefits to them?

_____

_____

_____

3. When you bless others, what are the benefits that return to you?

_____

_____

_____

4. How will you bless another person or persons?

_____

_____

_____

5. Make a list of some of the people in your life that you intend to bless.

_____

_____

_____

_____

_____

_____

Chapter Eight

A Time To Bless!

Words happen to be the containers in which blessings are given. When is the best time to empty these buckets of positive encouragements into the life of someone you desire to bless? The bottom line is that any time is a good time to bless others. However, there are specific times and wonderful occasions in life which just seem to be begging for the blessing to be shared.

There is a time for everything, and a season for every activity under heaven (Eccl. 3:1).

I remind you that the elements of a spoken blessing are to be positive, imparting a message that attaches a high value or "added value" to the one whom you are blessing. By faith, you impart a picture of a better future. The following are some meaningful times in life's junctures that are most appropriate to share a thoughtful blessing:

BEGIN AT THE BEGINNING—PREGNANCY:

Modern science has proven that the unborn child has an ability to receive messages or stimuli from outside the womb. This is a confirmation of a biblical truth we already know. Consider:

> *Before I formed you in the womb I knew you, before you were born I set you apart; I appointed you as a prophet to the nations"* (Jeremiah 1:5).

> *When Elizabeth heard Mary's greeting, the baby leaped in her womb, and Elizabeth was filled with the Holy Spirit . . . as soon as the sound of your greeting reached my ears, the baby in my womb leaped for joy* (Luke 1:41, 44).

I believe Mary greeted Elizabeth with a spoken greeting of blessing, and the baby responded! How fitting . . . a spoken blessing to the parents as well as to the unborn child. Talk about a great start in life. We can begin very early to shape a life with a blessing!

FOLLOW UP WITH A BIRTH AND BIRTHDAY BLESSINGS:

The biblical pattern begins to unfold before us as something good to follow. Start with Jesus Christ,

> *On the eighth day ... he was named Jesus, the name the angel had given him before he was conceived. Joseph and Mary took him to Jerusalem to present him to the Lord ... Simeon took him in his arms and praised God* (Luke 2:21-22, 28).

Simeon blessed the child Jesus and his parents, Joseph and Mary. Bless the child and bless the parents ...an excellent step because they all need it.

At the birth of John the Baptist, "Her [Elizabeth's] neighbors and relatives ... shared her joy" (Luke 1:58) as well as blessings and celebration.

Look at the life of Paul as he wrote about his gratitude with these words, "But when God, who set me apart from birth and called me by his grace ... " (Galatians 1:15).

Births and birthdays are wonderful and meaningful events on which to share a blessing. They're exactly the times to picture that special future!

THE WEANING OF A CHILD IS AN OFTEN OVER-LOOKED TIME TO BLESS:

This I discovered as a whole new possibility when I reread the book of Genesis. It had never occurred to me or maybe to you, either. Think about it. The taking away of the bottle or breast from a child who has grown very attached to food dispensed in these ways means that the child will not have the comfort this has afforded them. It can be a traumatic time, but another time to impart something special to a little one.

The pattern for such an event, or even a party, is also biblical:

The child grew and was weaned, and on that day Isaac was weaned, Abraham held a great feast (Genesis 21:8).

It does not specifically state that Abraham blessed the child, but we do know from Jewish culture and traditions that this was a time when the blessing played an important role. It's a milestone of separation and a first step toward maturity. Why not bless this time in the life of a child?

WHEN SCHOOL BEGINS:

Do you remember your first day of school? In the lives of our four kids, this proved to be a very traumatic event. It certainly could have gone much more smoothly with an appropriate blessing to begin a new era of living. Most kids sure could use some help in easing their fears of the unknown at school. Think of the new faces they will meet, the teachers they will face—it's a frightening situation to some young children. We could ease these times with special blessings! Likely there will be kindergarten plus twelve more "first" school days to bless!

This has possibilities whether your children attend public, private, parochial school, or even are home schooled. These all begin on a specific day and time.

THE "COMING-OUT EVENT" OF GROWING UP:

You may want to think in terms of puberty. But exactly when does this passing from an adolescent to become an adult happen? Most cultures worldwide have some sort of rite of passage, which too many of us in our Western culture have ignored.

The biblical pattern can be seen in the life of Jesus, "When he was twelve years old, they went up to the Feast, according to the custom" (Luke 2:42). I listened as a Jewish rabbi patiently explained that Jesus was, in reality, 13 years old because the Jews celebrate birthdays as beginning with conception. According to this, Jesus was nine months older than Luke wrote about him. Another explanation is that as a part of this Feast, Jesus was initiated into the adult community of faith in a "bar mitzvah" type of recognition.

The Jewish pattern is based on culture, custom, and tradition. There is a *bar mitzvah* for thirteen-year-old boys and a *bat mitzvah* for twelve-year-old girls. Publicly, in the presence of members of the synagogue, the parents and grandparents, as well as the rabbi, lay hands on these children and bless them. It's always followed by a party—a coming-out party where these children are welcomed to the adult world and are then treated as adults, with adult responsibilities from this point on.

In the life of Christ this event was another fulfillment of prophecy according to the prophet.

> *The Spirit of the Lord will rest on him ... the Spirit of wisdom and of understanding, the Spirit of counsel and of power, the Spirit of knowledge and of the fear of the Lord ... and he will delight in the fear of the Lord* (Isaiah 11:2).

There's another event that also takes place at the bar or bat mitzvah that is powerful! For each child a special "minion" is formed of ten trusted adults who are at least thirty years of age. They will serve this child until age thirty as mentors, meeting periodically with the child to help with every major decision of life. It's in this minion where logic is learned and Jewish practices of life and business are passed on. Parents take less a parenting role and the minion takes on more of the managing and mentoring along with the parents. It's very effective in the lifestyle of the Jewish community. They deal with questions such as, Whom do I marry? Where do I live? What shall I do with my life? Where shall I go to college? And many more.

An interesting side note: Jesus was considered age thirteen when he began his adult responsibility by spending it in the Father's house of worship. He was age thirty when he began his earthly ministry to the world. We assume the time from thirteen until age thirty was spent in becoming a mature adult under the mentoring of others.

WHEN THE YOUNG ADULT LEAVES THE NEST:

We well remember the subterfuge Jacob pulled on his aged father Isaac when stealing the blessing of the firstborn. However, we have mostly overlooked the special blessing Isaac gave to Jacob on the parting from his father's house. Let's read it:

So Isaac called for Jacob and blessed him and commanded him: "May God Almighty bless you and make you fruitful and increase your numbers until you become a community of peoples. May He give you and your descendants the blessing given to Abraham, so that you may take possession of the land where you now live as an alien" (Genesis 28:1, 3-4).

The Bible also records many more blessings spoken over children on the event of their leaving home. For example: Laban spoke blessings in Genesis 31:55; Jacob followed this pattern in Genesis 48 and 49 over his sons; Jethro spoke a blessing over his son-in-law Moses when he returned to Egypt; the family of Rebecca blessed her as she left home to become the bride of Isaac in Genesis 24:60; and there are many more biblical instances of this practice. When children leave home, think of their new challenges. The blessing of God can sure help as a confidence builder, as well as an encourager for a positive future!

A WEDDING IS ALWAYS A TIME TO BLESS:

Each of the foregoing events is important. But the marriage of two people may be the most important time for a blessing. The preacher almost always invokes a blessing. At the reception there is the occasion for others to bless the bride and groom.

The Bible makes a special promise: "Blessed are those who are invited to the wedding supper of the Lamb!" (Revelation 19:9). There's also another romantic, beautiful blessing at the wedding of Boaz and Ruth:

Then the elders and all those at the gate said, "We are witnesses. May the Lord make the woman who is coming into your home like Rachel and Leah, who together built up the house of Israel. May you have standing in Ephrathah and be famous in Bethlehem

through the offspring the Lord gives you by this young woman and may your family be like that of Perez, whom Tamar bore to Judah"
(Ruth 4:11-12).

AT MEMORABLE SPIRITUAL JUNCTURES:

This time of a spiritual turn-about or encounter with God or even an angelic ambush when a person might be surprised is a time to bless! What do I really mean? It's hard to put into words. Perhaps the juncture may be at a baptismal service, or following the dedication of your life to Christ, or when you have a spiritual experience you hadn't planned. These can all be times when you, in turn, bless the Lord!

Once more, Jacob is our example. He was forced to run for his life from his angry brother. And as he laid his head on a stone, God met him in a dream:

When Jacob awoke from his sleep, he thought, "Surely the Lord is in this place, and I was not aware of it." He was afraid and said, "How awesome is this place! This is none other than the house of God (Bethel); this is the gate of heaven" (Genesis 28:16-17).

In the life of Mary, mother of Jesus, after the visitation of the angel, she responded with a magnificent blessing which we call the "Magnificat" or the song of Mary.

Saul the persecutor had a "Damascus" road experience and changed his name to Paul. He spent a lifetime changed, as a blesser of others.

AFTER MILESTONE ACHIEVEMENTS:

Jesus told a parable in which servants were given five talents, two talents, and one talent. Then the master went on a journey. And after quite some time, he returned to make an accounting. Two of these servants had doubled their money—ten talents and four talents. One still had his single initial one. Two were blessed because of their achievement:

> *Well done, good and faithful servant! You have been faithful with a few things. Come and share your master's happiness* (Matthew 25:21,23).

Why not give someone a blessing after a job well done? Why not give a blessing when a promotion has come? Why not do it when a new discovery has been accomplished? Why not bless someone when a new job has been offered to them?

WHEN SICKNESS OR PHYSICAL NEEDS STRIKES:

Abraham's wife, Sarai, had a need—she was now

old and well beyond the age of childbearing, yet there was the promise of God to build a great nation of people from her and her husband. What happened?

As for Sarai your wife, you are no longer to call her Sarai; her name will be Sarah. I WILL BLESS HER and will surely give you a son by her. I will bless her so that she will be the mother of nations (Genesis 17:15-16).

Did God heal her or bless her? Interesting. I believe that the blessing brought the healing.

Then we have the story of King Hezekiah who was terminally ill. This king called on God for help and healing. Isaiah was sent to bring words of blessing and in three days the king was healed!

I have heard your prayer and seen your tears; I will add fifteen years to your life (Isaiah 38:5).

Words of blessing are powerful as in:

The words I have spoken to you are spirit and they are life (John 6:63).

EVERY SUNDAY OR SABBATH DAY CELEBRATION:

We think of each Hebrew Sabbath celebration as a special time. Traditionally and culturally as part of this celebration, parents bless their children in the name of the God of Abraham, Isaac, and Jacob. When they gather as a congregation in a Sabbath celebration, as part of the service, the children are generally blessed by the elders and rabbi. How about doing the same kind of thing in our Christian celebrations? It could become a wonderful, exciting habit.

HOW ABOUT MAKING EVERY HOLIDAY CELEBRATION A TIME OF BLESSING?

Here again, think of the possibilities! It's simply another time to share a blessing. Think of the calendar. There's New Year's, President's Day, Easter, Memorial Day, and on and on. If nothing more, simply use the priestly blessing from Numbers chapter six.

WHEN RETIREMENT LOOMS:

Biblically there is no such thing as a retirement celebration. In fact, the Bible never speaks of a time when you can begin to take life easy. So really, we don't have a pattern there. However, we do live in a society when age sixty-five means you can stop your employment and do something different with the remainder of your life. This can be a traumatic time because of the radical life changes involved. A positive time of blessing could surely add value to this new era of living.

WHEN DEATH APPROACHES:

Who wants to talk about death and dying? Not many of us! However, not a single one of us will escape this world alive. It's a reality that cannot be denied.

Once more we use the life of Jacob as our example. At the close of his life, this man, who had made blessing such a part of his existence, concludes his life with a time of blessing his sons and grandsons (Genesis 49).

Isaac, when he is old and anticipating his home going prepared himself to pronounce the blessings on his two sons, Jacob and Esau.

King David is seen as giving last minute blessings and instructions to his son Solomon who succeeded him as the king.

Jesus prepared His disciples for their life ahead without Him by pronouncing many blessings on these followers (Luke 24).

Paul the Apostle wrote a number of letters to his followers while in prison awaiting his execution.

Some of the most meaningful words of a lifetime have been spoken as a last will and testament. Parting words are not easily forgotten.

You might be thinking, "That's sure a lot of blessing!" Yes, it is and it should be. Giving blessings to others needs to be a lifestyle that we live. And then you also may be thinking, "I'm not that creative to keep thinking of new and exciting blessings." Repetition is fine; in fact it's wonderful! Blessings are worth repeating. We need to drive this truth home. How often did the Israelites hear the priestly blessing of Numbers 6 pronounced over them? How else will you mark others with the name of God?

There are two interesting ancient Jewish fables that illustrate the truth of the need to bless. The first rabbi questioned God about the high priestly blessing: "Why should I bless Your people when You can do it so much better?" God replied that he should do it because He commanded the rabbi to bless, but then reminded the rabbi that He was always present in the blessing, imparting His life to His people in the blessing!

The other old rabbi said to his students, "Bless people the day before you die."

"But, rabbi," replied the student, "I don't know the day I will die."

"Then, bless the people today!"

YOU CAN ALSO BLESS YOURSELF!

The Bible commands us to "bless and do not

112

curse." We normally believe this applies to our interaction with others. But what kind of self-talk do you direct toward yourself? Why not take this as a directive for you, personally? Again, you have the choice to bless or curse!

May I suggest the following as a guide in beginning to bless yourself?

• I declare I am blessed with supernatural wisdom and clear directions for my life and my future!

• I declare I am blessed with a strong will, self-control, self-discipline as well as courage and ability to move into a brighter future!

• I declare I am blessed with success, strength, promotion, and God's divine protection!

• I declare that any curse spoken over me, any evil discouraging words spoken over me, and any actions of a curse modeled for me, are broken in Jesus' powerful name.

• I declare that I am blessed with Abraham's blessing which is provided to me by the sacrifice of Jesus Christ, and now I am free of all past family or generational curses!

The biblical basis for such declarations is written for each of us in the writings of Paul the Apostle:

Christ redeemed us from the curse of the law by becoming a curse for us ... He redeemed us

113

in order that the blessing given to Abraham might come to the Gentiles through Christ Jesus, so that by faith we might receive the promise (Galatians 3:13-14).

I would like to conclude with this special blessing for you.

BE BLESSED WITH . . .

• Promotion and God's favor!

• Be blessed in the city or in the country, wherever you live!

• Be blessed with abundance, growing enterprises and greater dreams!

• Be blessed with quality results, great, prosperous travels, and always a wonderful homecoming!

• Be blessed with victories in all of your life's battles and deliverance from all your enemies!

• Be blessed with overflowing storehouses, prosperous ventures and productive lands!

• Be blessed with sanctification and a calling by the Name of God!

• Be blessed with physical security, peace in your spirit, timely rains of blessing, and meaningful work!

• Be blessed so that you can eliminate all need to borrow and instead be a lender!

• Be blessed with leadership and success in all phases of your life!

• Be blessed with God's favor as well as the favor of mankind!

I have just blessed you with the twenty-eight bountiful blessings from Deuteronomy 28:1-21!

SELF-GUIDED STUDY

The Word of God contains everything we need to know to be blessed by Him and to pass the blessing on to others. It's a subject that's ultimately broader than the scope of this book. Do you realize that the words bless, blessed, blessedness, blessings, blessest and blesseth are found more than 500 times in the Bible? It's a huge subject that needs more study. So, I would encourage you to continue. The following will be a start.

1. What it means to be blessed

Genesis 1:22, 28; 12:2-3; Proverbs 10:22; Galatians 3:13-14

My thoughts:

_____

_____

_____

_____

_____

_____

_____

_____

_____

_____

_____

2. The blessing and temptation

James 1:12

My thoughts:

_____

_____

_____

_____

_____

_____

_____

_____

_____

_____

_____

3. The blessing and the Bible

James 1:25

My thoughts:

_____

_____

_____

_____

_____

_____

_____

_____

_____

_____

_____

4. The blessing and listening to God

Proverbs 8:32-34

My thoughts:

_____

_____

_____

_____

_____

_____

_____

_____

_____

_____

_____

5. The blessing and living in obedience

Deuteronomy 28:1-14

My thoughts:

_____

_____

_____

_____

_____

_____

_____

_____

_____

_____

6. The curse and living in disobedience

Deuteronomy 28:15-48

My thoughts:

_____

_____

_____

_____

_____

_____

_____

_____

_____

_____

_____

7. The blessing and prosperity

Deuteronomy 30:1-10

My thoughts:

_____

_____

_____

_____

_____

_____

_____

_____

_____

_____

_____

8. The blessing and life or death

Deuteronomy 30:11-20

My thoughts:

_____

_____

_____

_____

_____

_____

_____

_____

_____

_____

_____

9. The blessing and God's favor

Psalms 5:12

My thoughts:

_____

_____

_____

_____

_____

_____

_____

_____

_____

_____

_____

10. The blessing and the fear of God

Psalms 115:12-16; 128:1-6; 112:1-10

My thoughts:

_____

_____

_____

_____

_____

_____

_____

_____

_____

_____

_____

11. The blessing and the counsel of the ungodly

Psalm 1:1-6

My thoughts:

_____

_____

_____

_____

_____

_____

_____

_____

_____

_____

_____

12. The blessing and trusting God

Psalms 2:12; 34:8; 40:4

My thoughts:

---

13. The blessing and right living

Psalm 106:3

My thoughts:

_____

_____

_____

_____

_____

_____

_____

_____

_____

_____

14. The blessing and integrity

Proverbs 20:7

My thoughts:

_____

_____

_____

_____

_____

_____

_____

_____

_____

_____

_____

15. The blessing and the poor

Psalm 41:1-2

My thoughts:

_____

_____

_____

_____

_____

_____

_____

_____

_____

_____

_____

16. The blessing and giving

Proverbs 10:22; Malachi 3:10; I Kings 17:8-12

My thoughts:

_____

_____

_____

_____

_____

_____

_____

_____

_____

_____

_____

17. The blessing and your harvest

Malachi 3:11-12

My thoughts:

_____

_____

_____

_____

_____

_____

_____

_____

_____

_____

_____

18. The blessing and spiritual blessings

Ephesians 1:3

My thoughts:

---

19. The blessing and faithfulness

Proverbs 28:20

My thoughts:

_____

_____

_____

_____

_____

_____

_____

_____

_____

_____

_____

_____

20. The blessing and putting God first

Matthew 6:33; Psalm 37:23;

My thoughts:

_____

_____

_____

_____

_____

_____

_____

_____

_____

_____

_____

21. The blessing and seeking God

Psalm 119:1-2; Matthew 5:6

My thoughts:

_____

_____

_____

_____

_____

_____

_____

_____

_____

_____

_____

22. The blessing and walking in love

I Peter 3:9; I Corinthians 3:8

My thoughts:

_____

_____

_____

_____

_____

_____

_____

_____

_____

_____

23. The blessing and the words of prophecy

Revelation 1:1-3

My thoughts:

_____

_____

_____

_____

_____

_____

_____

_____

_____

_____

_____

24. The blessing and how to pass it on to another person

Numbers 6:22-27; Genesis 24:59-60; 25:5; 47:7; 48:15-20; 49:1-28

My thoughts:

_____

_____

_____

_____

_____

_____

_____

_____

_____

_____

25. The blessing and Jesus Christ

Luke 2:22-32; Matthew 5:1-12; Mark 10:14; Luke 24:50-51

My thoughts:

_____

_____

_____

_____

_____

_____

_____

_____

_____

_____

26. The blessing and when you are cursed

I Corinthians 4:12, 16

My thoughts:

_____

_____

_____

_____

_____

_____

_____

_____

_____

_____

_____

27. The blessing and YOU

Romans 12:14; Galatians 3:13-14, 26-29; Genesis 12:2; 24:1

My thoughts:

_____

_____

_____

_____

_____

_____

_____

_____

_____

_____

_____

The LORD bless you

and keep you;

The LORD make His face

shine upon you

and be gracious to you;

The LORD turn His face

toward you and give

you peace!

(Numbers 6:24-26)

About the Author

ROBERT STRAND is the author of more than 60 books, and his "Moments To Give" series has sold more than five million copies. A consummate storyteller, Robert knows how to blend the emotional impact of true stories with practical insights from his many years of pastoral experience to produce breakthrough results. He and his wife, Donna, live in Springfield, Missouri.

To Book Robert Strand...

Robert Strand's books have inspired millions. As one of America's foremost story tellers, his "Moments" books have become favorites for gifts. He is also a popular public speaker doing church events as well as secular conventions.

Robert Strand is also available to present writer's conferences or seminars. You can book him for a personal speaking appearance by calling 417-883-4184 or 888-389-0225.

Books by Robert J. Strand
from Evergreen Press

These books can be purchased at your local bookstore or online at Amazon.com, BN.com, ChristianBook.com or call 888-670-7463

The Power of Forgiving
True stories of practical instruction to help you deal with irritations, heal relational breaks and forgive the "unforgivable." 1-58169-050-9 96 p $5.99

The Power of Thanksgiving
Time to take inventory of your blessings and begin a new lifestyle of Thanksgiving. 1-58169-054-1 96 p $5.99

The Power of Gift Giving
Learn how to give the intangible parts of your life and become a source of blessing to others.
1-58169-055-X 96 p $5.99

The Power of Motherhood
Mothers have a unique job today and the author shares insights and stories that encourage mothers to be all they can be. 1-58169-094-0 96 p $5.99

The Power of Fatherhood
Fathers also have a challenging job in turbulent times, and Strand share twenty stories about fathering that speak to dads. 1-58169-095-9 96 p $5.99

The Power of Grandparenting
What a wonderful delight and privilege it is to be a grandparent in today's world! Here are heartwarming stories that show us how to significantly conribute to one another's lives. 1-58169-156-4 96 p $5.99

Angel at My Door
More than 25 real-life angel encounters to warm the heart and point the reader to the God who loves us so much that He sends His messengers at critical times to protect, defend and encourage us.
1-58169-114-9 120 p $10.95

The B Word
A "blessing" can transform your life and the lives of those close to you. It's an extremely effective pronouncement that imparts hope, emotional healing, financial prosperity, longevity, and a multitude of other blessings. The power of the blessing transforms the lives of those who give it—and those who receive it! *The B Word* is filled with examples from the author's own family. Find out how you can minister the blessing to your family today.
1-58169-182-3 160 p $10.99